Top Sales Economic Strategies - 2014
How to Win the Customer's Business.

By

Larry Spates.

Publisher: Larry Spates

Clemmons, NC

Lspates777@gmail.com

Table of Contents

I would like to acknowledge

All of my many mentors who have been an inspiration to me in my sales career. To my many coworkers in sales, many Authors who's Books, Tapes, DC's and DVD trainings has been a blessing to me over the many years I have been in sales. To all of the customers over the years who took the time out their day to set and listen to my presentations and made a purchase of a product or service from me, and the companies I work with.

Special Thanks

To my Mother Mrs. Anna Jones Payne, who help me along the way with many encouraging words to stay in the fight and give it your all? Mr. Tom Cox for his time an attention helping me get a clear understanding of the Orkin Inc. Sales Program. The best approach to selling, as my mentor. Cedric Moser, My very good friend of many years and Sales Manager at Rent-A-Center.

To all of the employees who set in my sales department over the years listening and learning from the sales and management training I learned from others before, applying it to their sales careers, Miss. Dominique Hill, and Mrs. Erica Thompson for being two of the best administrative assistances that ever work for me. Mr. Stephen Edwards, Mr. Franky Alcorn, two of my top revenue producers in my sales department over and over again whom it was a pleasure to work with.

Mr. Patrick Smith, Who filled in when I was in the field with salesmen or in a training or management meeting. Mr. David Fulton, Miss. Sharee Plamer, Miss Anne Marie Rossi, very hard working call center service consultants, in one of the best outbound call center's in America.

Dedication

To my very good friend and employee the late Mr. Von Monday, who all always came into my office with a smile on his face and kind words of encourage wisdom.

Von would ask me every time he saw me, boss man how are you doing to day, always very sincere and concerned about my well being, and had an appreciation for the opportunity to be apart of our sales team at Home Team Pest Defense Inc.

Introduction

I have spent many days, weeks, months, and years in the business of selling, and I can truly tell you it has been one of the best decisions I ever made.

It's a pleasure to reach out and help people make the best purchasing decisions, and feel good about the products and services that has added value to their lives and that of their families.

After many years of selling and helping so many people I wanted to set down and share my thoughts and ideas on the subject of selling, ways to help thoughts who is come after me make the best of every opportunity they may have to help someone with a need of a company's products or services.

There is no business that will reward you like the business of selling, and nothing more rewarding than knowing you have given your very best and at the end of the day another customer has said I appreciate your help.

Sales is about helping people get the things they want at a fair price with great results in the products and services we sell, along with top quality customer service from the businesses we sell for.

So set back and get a pin, paper and a highlighter as we take a short journey down this road of sales and customer care.

Sales Success: What Is It All About?

Within you are the keys to your success:

(From The Ancient Scroll Mark III) In OG Mandino's: The Greatest Salesman In The World.

I will persist until I succeed.
I was not delivered into this world in defeat, nor does failure course in my veins. I am not a sheep waiting to be prodded by my shepherd. I am a loin and I refuse to

talk, to walk, to sleep with the sheep. The slaughterhouse of failure is not my destiny. I will persist until I succeed".

Many people ask the question how I can be successful. Where do I find the road that leads to a better life? Or why is it that some people have all of the luck and I can hardly get by?

It's all in the way that you think. The late Earl Nightingale said that man becomes what he thinks about most of the time. So become what you want to become by changing the way you think, or what you are thinking about.

So then if this is true what are you thinking? Your thoughts should line up with the desires of heart, along with the goals and dreams you are working to achieve. Thoughts are the ideas and actions that form within your mind regarding who you are and what you are purposed to accomplish while here on this planet we all call earth.

What is your purpose and how can you go about finding it? I believe that we all are created for a purpose while being here on earth, have you ever ask yourself what I'm I here to do. How do I go about making a difference? You are a unique person; with gifts and talents that no other person on this earth has to give. There is a place that only you fit; it's in the power of your heart, soul, and mind; you must search within you to find and understand your created purpose.

I began to search my mind and heart to see what I was created to do; after a numbers of years I found out that every person on this earth is born with a bent; some call it certain gifts; talents. We all have different gifts that were given to us at birth; we must get busy using these gifts, or we will lose them.

To find out what your special talent or gift is, ask you a simple question? What is the one thing I enjoy doing the most? It's not work for me; and I love doing it. Think about that for a moment. Now ask yourself when I get out of bed everyday what is it that I want to spend my life doing? When all you think about is this one thing, morning, noon, and night, you will have found your purpose in life. When you find your purpose; get busy doing that and your world will come alive.

I believe that in order to know and understand our purpose in life we must have a connection with our creator, some of us call him God, others may say our soul or spirit man within us.
Nevertheless we all have to be connection to the divine power, will in order to get in touch with our inter self.

I found that as I set quietly and meditate thoughts and ideas fill my mind and heart on things I need to take action on, when I act the results have always been just what I expected them to be. As I focus on a positive out come things always fall into place doors would open and new opportunities would always be waiting for me.

I remember once I was out of work for a long period of time, I filled out applications all over the city, then I changed my focus begin to apply this process and tool call thinking first and then acting, and new ideas jumped into my mind, so I acted upon them and landed a new job in a different field; I have been working in this field now for over 15 years. Someone said that man only uses about 10% of his mind or thinking ability, I have come to believe this is true.

What is it that you want to do with your life? Have you truly given it sincere thought?

I Have Been In Sales Since 1980 Right After I finished High School.

I have helped many people make purchasing decisions on products and services. Knives, Real Estate, Cell Phones, Cable, Home Phones, Furniture, Pest Control, Cars, Wireless Internet and much more.

I started as a salesman in a local Grocery Store called Great American Food Store. My first employer was a man name Mr. Jay Martin and from there my sales career started, I learned the value importance of every person that walked into that store, they were the ones who kept our doors opened and paid our salaries every week. From this small start I begin to help people get the things they wanted. As the years went by I worked my way up to sales manager, and board chairman within several companies I worked with. Over the years I have learned a lot about customer service.

As a manager in sales I ran the operations for a customer care call center training their customer service consultants the value of great customer communications and increase company sales and revenue growth and our sales team receive achieved top honors for a new record top revenue in 2010. I believe it's important for a sale manager to know and do the job better than every employee he or she hires. So I made my personal goal to learn every job in every role in hired an employee to do as a manager, from data entry to writing sales documents, whatever position I filled I new the 10 times better than the employee I hired and I goal was to make them better as a customer service consultant than I was.

I also worked in the field outside training our sales team who worked for me how to become the very best sale people in the business. One hour a day five days a week I did sales training with my team, teaching them how to become the very best listeners, coaching them on how to help the customer make purchasing decisions that would give them the most value for their investment.

Many people who worked for me then now work for companies all across America as sales manager, some even started their own business.

I have worked for some of the best companies, and some of the worse companies in America.

I have had some of the top salesmen and women work with and for me. Not once did I ever expect anything from them that I could not do myself. Nor did I ever set unfair objectives and goals that I knew that I myself could not meet or reach. I know in my heart that is was not right, and why would expect my sales people to go out and do it. Sales people are professional business men and women not your children sales manager, and should they be treated as the professionals they are.

Some companies set the worse goals and objectives for their sales force and wonder why they receive the results to get. The question I always ask myself is it fair to my sales team? Am I willing to get out on the front lines at the time I have ask them to be out? Is every condition a good one and will they be safe in the field? If not I got to management and fight for what's fair and right for my people. Sales manager it's your responsibility to care of and look out for your people, this is why you were hired in the first place. Some sales managers are robots and whatever management says goes. many of these companies are no longer in business today because of how they treated their people, and felt it was good business, then passed that treatment down to their customers.

Every sale that a salesperson makes is new revenue a company earns, and that being the case, why do companies refuse to pay their sales force all commissions for their work?

When my sales team made a sale I paid them for that sale because it was the right thing to do. Each sales person had a quota to meet every month, but I always paid my team members for every single sale brought into the company on top of their salary.

No one wants to work and not be compensated for their efforts, any company that refuses to pay their sales force for every sale is stealing from it's sales team. It's just bad business not to pay a sales people unless they hit a quota. Sales manager if a sales person is not where he or she needs to be for the month help them, or release them, but for the love of God stop stealing their commissions. It's just another excuse used by companies to keep commissions and make their bottom live revenue look good. Stop playing the role of the devil; he too comes to steal anything he can get his hands on.

This could also be the reason some companies are just getting by, they are loosing business as fast as they earn new business, they make 5 sales and loose twice and many customers the same day. If you are loosing business as fast as you are gaining it something wrong with the way you treat your employees or your customers, and in some case both are being mistreated by bad management. Sale people if you work for one of these employers leave and go where you are appreciate for your talent as well as your efforts.

Sales managers could never demand and thing from their people, but commanded it by their own willingness to be a true team player. Sales manager you can not lead where you have never been, and you can not show what you don't know, you are only fooling yourself.

In the arm forces of the United States of America, every man and woman goes through the same training.

They fully understand what their call of duty and service is to our country. They also meet every requirement of their leading commander, who have also done what is required of them, that's what makes our arm forces here in this country so great.

Only poor company management promotes people within the company that does not qualify with proper skills and training to move forward.

When trained person come into an untrained environment within a company, they know and can clearly see what is going on. It don't take very long before untrained people in leadership see them as a treat, and start mistreating them with write ups, performance issues, and finally forcing them out the door to save and protect their own job.

Many times the real result is that these businesses close their doors, and never really knew what happened to them simply because someone looking out for a friend or co-worker who really never qualified for a management position within their business was promoted and had no business in leadership and as result the entire company paid the price for it.

The Customer Service You Give Will Make or Close Your Business.

No matter what a company sells, it's the people on the front lines that keep the doors open within and company. Customer service is key and company life or destruction in business. When a customer buy your products or services they invest in and trust what you have told them and it's you responsibility to stand up and keep your word.

When there is a concern with a product or service you sold to a customer stop everything and make it right with that customer. It's not products that cost businesses to close their doors, it's the poor quality service they give the customer when they call or return with problems with the products and services they purchased. It's only takes a few minutes to fix a problem or at least let the customer know you are working to resolve an issue or concern they have. There is a saying, it goes like this " Do unto others as you would have them do unto you" don't ever let a customer walk away angry with you or a product you sold them fix it or refund their money. It's as simple as that, I just don't want to make a customer happy at the time of the sale, but I want them to keep coming back to make purchasing decision to buy from me because I " Take Care of The Customer" every time there is a problem.

Always hire people with a heart and compassion for others, if they have an I don't care attitude send them out the door of your business, if they are unhappy with their job responsibilities as a customer service consultant, let them know in a very nice way that you fully understand how they feel, and you are not upset with them, you only want what is best for them. Make it simple, tell them you are releasing them to go do

what makes them happy, but get them out of your place of business.

I remember when I worked for United Parcel Service many years ago I was trained the value of a customer and how to give top quality customer service.
We had a program called next day air service. It was and still is a top quality service at UPS. There are two priority service times that every driver must meet with their customers daily. 10:30 am, by 12pm Next Day Air Deliveries. These customers paid a premium for their packages, every drive know the value of this service to the customer. These packages are delivered before anyone else receives anything off of our deliver trucks. What am I saying? it's simple, "take care of the customer", and they will take care of you.

I remember when i started driving for UPS there was a local business that had open on Peterscreek Parkway in Winston-Salem NC it is call the Market Place Mall. Years ago when I delivered the Market Place Mall it had over 30 stores at that location. I made a visit by the Market Place Mall a few months ago and there were only Three stores there from over 25 years ago when I delivered packages for UPS. The Dress Barn, **Abundant Life** Vitamins & Herbs and Burlington Shoes. Now my question is what happened to all of the other businesses at the Market Place Mall. Many of them are out of business because they forgot the most important thing and that is to take care of the customer, many of whom took there business somewhere else.

Customer service department will make or destroy a company, believe me I have seen many company lose tons of customers because of poor and untrained customer service reps. When I shopped for a product one thing I keep in mind is who will help me when I walk into a store, or will I speak to when I pick up the phone and call into a company about a problem I am having with their product or service. I have left many companies because of poor customer service. Another thing I learned is you can tell the quality of service you will receive from a company by the way their sales force treat you at the time of the sale. You can also tell what kind of service you will receive by the way companies treat their employees. If they trash their employees they will trash you too.
If they disrespect their employees in front of you can expect the same when doing business with them.

I have been trained by the best companies in the sales business and services business. UPS, Rollins Inc, Clearwire Inc, Hosanna House of Transition Inc. I have also received top quality sales training courses, One of the very best, Mazda Inc, Ron Willinham's Integrity Selling, Selling In Turbulent Times, Orkin Sales and Management, just to name a few. I have read and listened to some of the very best authors on sales leadership and development. Such as Anthony Robins - Personal Power, Tom Rath - Strength Finder, Daniel C. Matt - The ZOHAR. Dale Carnegie – Sell Like A Pro, Norman Vincent Peal – The Power of Positive Thinking, and my daily guide the Bible.

Five Secrets to Having a Successful Sales Career and a Lasting Business Relationship with Your Sales People and Your Customers.

1. Be an affective closer. Never forget, It's all in the close of the sale.
2. Know what you are paying your sales people to do, never steal a commission, sales people and management, your sales force will hate you for it and walk out when they get training to be successful. Pay your people for every sale they make.

3. Invest in top quality training systems and programs, A key to sales is never ever stop training your people. Sales people also should invest in their careers, go out and purchase sales programs, play them while you are driving to appointments.

4. Always be learning something about sales and customer service. Rule to remember people love to talk about themselves, and they love the sound of their name, it's like magic to their ears, it's not

about you sales person, it's about them. " Take Care of The Customer"

5. Create a strong and effective customer friendly organization. Build your own network and customer referral data base. It will be the life of your sales career, let everyone you meet know what you do for a living, give them 2 business cards, one for them and another one to give a family member or friend, and also as for a referral. People by buy from people they have relationships with. Start with the people you already have relationships with, you family and friends, don't tell anyone but these are the key secrets to your sales success in this business.

Three of the Most Important Things I Learned About Sales, and Continue to Use Daily.

1. The Importance of The People Who Work for You.

I learned that the most important people in sales are the people on the front lines, my employees. They work hard and long hours going from door to door, picking up the phone hour after hour making calls to people they have never seen, willing to do everything in a respectable way to bring in new business for the company.

Always show kindness and respect to your sales team, never put them down or degrade them because you are having a bad day or the sales numbers are not what you want them to be. When my sales team struggled I picked up the phone and made calls and closed sales myself to help the team get to our goal for the day, week and month. If an outside sales person needed my help I would go out with him we worked together and stopped had lunch together I paid for it with my own money, not a company card because I had that much respect for the people who worked for me. Our sales people are a prize possession and jewels to our company.

I always made selling as fun as I could for my sales team. Once a week I would set a daily goal for seasoned sales people, and my new hires and gave them gift cards when they reached their goals, everyone had a chance to reach the top. When I saw the team being burned out, I would just stop in the middle of the day, load everyone up in our cars and go have lunch. We would take time to relax and enjoy selling, and we exceeded our goals every month. I went out of my way to take care of my people, when they performed well, I gave them gift cards, lunch and dinners as a team not just to the a top performer, because it took the entire team to reach our goals. When you take care of your people you will be amaze what they will do for you.

2. The Importance of Quality Products and Services.

Good products carry a weight of gold in companies that understand the importance of having products and service that are top quality. People will spread the word about your products and services when they are pleased, and send you referral business as a result of their experience with your company's products or services. Nothing beats a top quality line of products that people need and are willing to pay premium price for.

No matter how good a sales person may be if the products and services they are selling do not meet the needs of the customer they are in front of it's a waste of their time.

Time Management:

Time is one of the most important things in life we have and the way we use it makes all of the difference in this world if you are going to be successful in sales.

I always think about the time I have in a given day and how it can be used to benefit me most.

I have learn to break my day down in three ways as a sales manager.

1. Things I need to finish from the day before. I set 2 hours first thing every day after all employees are settled, and have every thing they need to start their work day.
 I take this time to complete all paper work, respond to emails, letters and notes or any thing I need to do that requires me to write or complete any service agreement or document.

2. I attend all meetings within the office I need to be in, or any meeting I have with an employee, I set aside 2 hours for in house meetings.

3. Last I take all movements trips, 1 hour or longer if needed to go to the post office meet a tech in the field handle customer service issues and take a lunch break or appointment. outside meeting or other business such as make bank deposits, all movements are done last. I take lunch return to the office, work with my sales team and start the same process in the afternoon until time to go home.   This system has same me a lot of time during the run of a business day, and I use it at home as well. It works wonders for managing your time.

Setting Goals:

Goal setting is essential to any successful sales career, without goal there is no direction or way to determine what a sales person has or is trying to accomplish.

Goals should be measurable and attainable, they should make sense and one should set small goals and then as they reach them begin a new goal. Start with weekly goals, then set a goal for 30 days, 90 days, 6 months and then 1 year, 5 years, 10 years based on where you want to be and accomplish in that time frame.

You must also write out your goals and read them daily so that you can stay on track, focusing on the goal at hand. You might want to share a goal with a friend or a family member that will remind you and check your progress as to where you are and how many day you have left to reach your goal.

Write out a plan in small steps that you can use to take action everyday until your goal is realized and you have met the time span you set to complete it.
 The only way you are going to have any result in this area of your life is to make up your mind to take action and to do.

Many people want to change, but it will only happen when you get up and do something to bring about the change you want to see. Talk is cheap, not taking positive actions to get the results you desire or reach the dreams in your heart it starts when you get up and get moving in the direction you wish to go. Things don't change people change things and habits in their own lives. Start today, simply set a goal and take the first step to see your dream come true. If it's to be it's up to you.

The Cold Call:

It's not easy to make a cold call on the phone or in person, but it has to be done, I think the best part of making the call is getting into the right mind set. Prepare yourself for the call or visit. People are not expecting to see or hear from you. Rule number 1.Put a pleasant smile on your face. Rule number 2, Before you call, knock or ring their door bell remember it's about them not you, Rule number 3. find common ground to talk about with them, you only have 5 seconds to make a good first impression so don't waste time thinking about what to say, you should ready to talk with them. Rule number 4. Relax and speak in a soft tone of voice, introduce yourself and your company, if in person show your ID and speak as if you are talking with someone you have known all of your life, never appear frightened or afraid, even though they don't know you, they will respect the fact that you stopped by to help them, ask them their name and use it through out the entire conversation with them.

A persons name is music to their soul, always use their name. Rule number 5. build rapport with the person, ask them about themselves, what they do for a living? how long they have been doing that? How do they like it? Ask about their family, awards, vehicles you may see in the driveway, whatever keeps the attention on them. Once you have gotten them to relax and listening to you.

Next: Move into the reason for your visit. Why are you here is the question in their mind? So ask them an opened ended question regarding ways to help them get the most investment value for the money they spend on company products and services? And them say Mr. Williams would you be open to discuss some ways I may be able to save you money on the product or service you are doing presentations on? Let them answer you and then respond.

3. Take Care of The Customer.

I have had many experiences in this business call sales, but one thing to remember, always plan to succeed, and you will. To succeed I must take care of every customer.

Joe Girard, the world's greatest car salesman is one of my favorite sales mentors. I listen to a lot of the sales trainings Joe recorded, and one thing I learned from him is to always "take care of the customer".

I work for a local company doing door to door sales. One afternoon I knock on the door of an older lady Miss. Linda, she opened the door she was a very small frail looking lady, she ask me how can I help you? I told her who I was and who I worked for showed her my company badge, and ask her if she was happy with her service provider at the time? Her reply was yes and I'm in a contract. I ask if she was pleased with the service? She said yes.

I responded Miss. Linda I want to leave some information with you, and if anything should change with your service company please give me a call. She said I will do that, and closed her door. I walk away to the next unit in the complex I was working, and continued down the street as I was walking back to my car I heard this very soft voice say Mr. Larry I said yes, It was Miss. Linda, and she ask if I had a moment to speak to her? I said yes and she invited me in.

We discussed her current service provider, she was not very happy at all with the experience she was having. I told her about our service and the plan that would fix her needs, she reminded me that she had just renewed her contract with the company a month earlier but was not happy, I responded that I understood her concerns. Miss. Linda ask if I could stop by on the next day she had a family member that was to arrive soon and did not want to continue the discussion at that point.

I set up an appointment for 2pm the next day and thanked her for listening to my presentation. The following day at 12:30 pm I received a call but was in a meeting and could not answer, but after the meeting I listened to the voice mail and it was a reminder call from Miss. Linda about the 2pm appointment I had set up with her. I called her back to confirm I would be there. I left my sales meeting and drove 30 minutes to make the appointment. Miss. Linda had decided to accept my presentation and go with our service company. There was only cone condition and that was that I had to be at her home when she called the other service company to cancel their service. I said I can do that for you. So I completed all of the investment documentation paperwork and thanked Miss. Linda for her business, set up a time and date for the installation of services and a follow up appointment which we agreed she would call cancel her service with her other service provider which was doing my follow up visit.

On the morning the service was to be completed our tech was running behind and called to inform the customer, she also called me and I also called to ensure the customer that everything would be fine. I later received another call from Miss. Linda that she had only gotten part of the service completed and the tech would have to return at a later date. Once again I stopped by my customer's home to reassure her that everything was going to work out just fine.

While talking with Miss. Linda on this visit she decided to call and cancel the service of the other service provider. I ask her to wait until everything was done by our company and she said no I want to cancel it now, so I set and listen as she made the call.

The other company did everything in it's power to hold on to Miss. Linda and even added a $ 220.00 dollar cancellation fee, she became so angry that she handed me her phone and said if you want my business you get this service canceled, thought to myself what?

I took the phone and ask to speak the customer service supervisor to which she agreed and place me on hold. The supervisor picked up the phone I explained to him all of the trouble Miss. Linda said was going on with the service, I concluded that the cancellation fee should be waved due to all of the problems the customer had experienced in the past few months and had just renewed a month earlier and was still having the same problems. The supervisor game me his name and the name of a compliance manager that would be calling Miss. Linda back in a couple of days. I ended the call with him and gave her the contact information I had written down while talking with the supervisor for their company.

A couple of evenings later Miss. Linda called me it was after 10pm I let the call go into the voice mail but later listen to it. Miss. Linda wanted a call back as soon as I got the message, so I called her back, and said hi Miss. Linda I am returning your call. Miss. Linda said Mr. Larry I want to thank you for handling that company for me, Their compliance manager called me back, canceled their service, wave the early termination fees of $ 220.00 and is mailing me the boxes to send them their equipment back. She said I need you to help me pack up the equipment when the boxes come, will you do that for me Mr. Larry? to which I replied yes I will Miss. Linda.

The boxes arrived a few days later I went back by the customer's home packed up the old equipment for her and took it to the post office and mailed it for her. Today I have a very happy customer, and sometime I still receive a call from Miss. Linda for the service I provided her during the sales process. One thing I learned, the sale is not over when the buying decision has been made by the customer.

Never walk away when the customer ask for your help, not only did I win a customer but I have another friend as a result of giving good customer service at the time of the sale.

"Take Care Of The Customer".

Think Before You Speak:

I have learned to use my power to think about subject matters before I answer any questions. We all have the power to think; I heard that man only uses about 10% of his mental abilities to do whatever he does in life; this might be because so many of us are reactive instead of being proactive. Proactive people are thinkers, they don't wait to react to any thing; they think about every thing and take action to stay ahead in live. There are three kinds of people in this world.

The people who make things happen; the peoples who watch things happen; and people who just wonder what happened. While of these are you; be a the BIG THINKER and create your own world of success, you have the power to make things happen in your favor; to build the kind of world you want to live in. I watch people all over the TV as they complain about the State of the Union; what the President has or has not done: our economy's condition; is the left correct? Or is it the right that is correct? Is the congress right? Or is it the senate? Sometime my head starts spending listening to all of this.

What really matter is are you making a real difference; or just caught up in the hoop la of the day? If you really want to help be a doer; get involved with some

great ideas that will change what you don't like; begin
by using you thinking tool; your mind.

(Dale Carnegie) In his Book "How to Win Friends and
Influence People"
 Tell us there are twelve ways to win people to you way
of thinking.
1. The only way to get the best of an argument is to
    avoid it.
2. Show respect for the other man's opinions. Never
    tell a man he is wrong.
3. If you are wrong, admit it quickly and
    emphatically.
4. Begin in a friendly way.
5. Get the other person saying "yes, yes"
    immediately.
6. Let the other man do a great deal of the talking.
7. Let the other man feel that the idea is his.
8. Try honestly to see things from the other
    person's point of view.
9. Be sympathetic with the other person's ideas and
    desires.
10. Appeal to the nobler motives.
11. Dramatize your ideas.
12. Throw down a challenge.

People will appreciate you better when they know
that you respect them and give them credit for being
who they are. No two people are alike in this world,
if we all acted the same, dressed the same, said all of

the same things, eat al of the same foods, what a dull world this would be. Let the world around you help you to develop and grow always be open and think with your whole heart and mind.

I saw a post hanging in my sister-in-laws living room that said "Our mind is like a parachute; it works better when open". Many times we tend to respond before we think, I guess we sometimes want to be first with and answer, or we might like to stand out; it's nothing wrong with standing out if we have the knowledge and the facts on what we are discussing and talking about.

Sometimes we may feel a need to run and share something we heard from a friend, family member, or even a co-worker, however we need to think about the people who might be affected by our comment. Is what we are about to share the truth? Do we have all of the facts straight? Will there be a back lash if our information or the source and references are flawed in anyway?

The point I'm making is it's easy to say something or share information we hear, it's even better when we can depend on our source and know that we have thought through the process and media outlet we have decided to use to send our messages into the air waves, local and foreign throughout the world.

We have so many channels of communication any more that we have to make sure all of our home work has been done and we are only sharing the facts.

A rule I learned years ago about sharing information: Is what I'm about to say going to be hurtful to anyone? If so I won't say it.

Is what I'm about to say going to breakup a home, marriage, and family or friend relationship? If so I won't speak it.

Is what I'm about to share going to bring harm or danger to another person's life? If so, I will not share it. As we think about our actions and consequences of our behavior, our attitude about many things will change for the better.

Some one once said "How many people will I meet today? How many lives will pass my way? I can help so many; I can help so much, if I greet each one with a gentle touch".

When we think first, we will make better decisions; we are more careful with the choice of words we use to express; there is a greater concern about the emotional state of the person we are trying to make a connection with. No matter what the subject matter, we also need to plan out ways to be most effective; what is the purpose for our talk; what are the goals we are trying to obtain on our topic; what result are we seeking to achieve; are we using the right approach? And have we thought out the direction we want to go with our subject.

When we think first, the out come can be much better: Good parents never discipline their children when they are highly angry, they understand that their emotions can create more harm than good when they are upset. They will wait until they are fully ready to approach the situation with the child and them sit down to have a conversation and discuss ways that will be best for the unwarranted actions or bad behaviors of their child or children.

When successful people make a decision to move forward on a project, all of the ground work has been laid out. They know all of the details of the process needed to complete their project; they have researched the cost, materials needed, time involved and the number of people it will take to get the project completed by the deadline time. Why is this? Because they have thought about every detail of their project.

The power of thought, the magic of the mind!
(Conair Byron)
Learning without thought is very hard on the mind; many people have to repeat
Or go back through programs; such as educational training; repeat grades in school, and job training programs because they refuse to use their brain to think.

Still many don't understand that it is very important to gather their thoughts before they take a hard fall on their face in front of fans, and groups of people that have gathered to see or hear what they have to say. There is no other way to prepare yourself for any concert; drama production; musical; become an actor or actress unless you have the will power to do what it takes to become the best and that is what becoming successful is really all about. Are you willing to pay the price of success?

There is another area that I think is very important to the success of every man, woman, boy, and girl, and that is relationships: how we see ourselves and then how we see others. Someone said you only get one chance to make a first impression with someone you meet for the first time.

From the time we meet someone we begin to size them up, we check out their clothes; hair style, their shoes, the way they talk, the things they may or may not say. It's all about what we would like for them to be in our mind. it's as if we make our own picture frame place it on a canvas put it on a wall; and then decide what we are going to put in the picture frame.

We decide how they should look; what they should be wearing, weather they should have on dress shoes, or a pair of tennis shoes; in others words, we might miss our blessing in building great friendships and relationships because instead of being a friend and be friendly we are too busy trying to build people into what we want to have hanging around our home and with us. Love accepts people as they are, and let them be themselves. True love is always looking for what it can do to improve current relationships and build new relationships; there are many kinds of boats and ships, but none as good as true friendship.

Ten Commandments of human relations.

1. Speak To People. There is nothing as nice as a cheerful word of greeting.
2. Smile at People. It takes 72 muscles to frown, only 14 to smile.
3. Call People by name. The sweetest music to anyone's ears if the sound of his / her own name.
4. Be Friendly and Helpful. If you would have friends, be a friend.
5. Be Cordial. Speak and act as if everything you do is a genuine pleasure.
6. Be genuinely interested in people. You can like almost everybody if you try.
7. Be Generous with praise- cautious with criticism.
8. Be Considerate with the feelings of others. There are usually three sides to a controversy; your, the other fellows, and the right side.
9. Be Alert to give service. What counts most in life is what we do for others.
10. Add to This a good sense of humor, a big dose of patience and a dash of humility, and you will be rewarded many-fold.

It's has been said by a number great authors that when you have respect for people and their options they will be more open and respectful to you, and listen to what you have to say.

Who Are The People You Talk With About Your Products and Services?

There are all kinds of people in this world and in the sales business you will meet all of them.
The main thing is that you learn as much a people as you can, the more you know about the person you are about to set down and talk with the better it will be for you and that person.

You must qualify the person you are about to help make a buying decision from you. Are they the decision maker for their household?
Is there any other person they need to consult with before they meet with you?
Do they own or have the right to make buying decisions for the home?

This all sounds simple but make sure you know whom you are speaking with. When I make a call or visit to Mr. Williams home I assume that Mr. Williams is the home owner and decision maker for his household, so when he answers the door or phone I simple confirm that.

Example: Hi my name is, I am with XYZ Company and I would like to speak with Mr. Roger Williams, Mr. Williams comes to the door or answers the phone, and says I am Roger Williams how make I help you? I have just confirmed who I am looking to speak with.

Know The Behavior Style Of The Person You Are Addressing:

Different people have their own way of communicating with the people they are about make a buying decision with. It's a good thing to know the different ways people think, and respond when spoken to. It's also a good thing to have a very good understanding of their personality style, the way they talk, act, the way they express themselves, when you tune into a person you can pick up a lot about them. How they speak, what they say, their body moments, hands are they crossed? Crossed means they are not very open to hear you. You need to gain more trust so built more rapport with them so that they will relax, and listen to what you have to say.

A smile from you may help, as you adjust your tone to match theirs, "here is a tip", when they breath and speak match their voice tone, and follow along with them, it's okay to respond the way they sound with the same tone of voice, lean forward just a bit when you know you have their attention, and stay on point with your conversation and business objective.

There are a number of different behavior styles out there, but I will share four of them with you, learn these and you will master every conversation you have with the buying power and decision makes that purchase your products and services.

1. The Talker- likes to hear himself, but will buy when listens to.
2. The Action Taker – Always ready to take action when he hears the right words and prices.
3. The Supporter – Needs help making decisions.
4. The Deep Thinker – Very busy, and just wants the facts but will always get back to you with his decision.

1. There is the person who likes to talk, The Talker: "The Talker"
The talker will share as well as listen to what you have to say, they have lots of awards and achievements to show you. Talk with them about their achievements, let them become comfortable with you and move into the reason for your visit.

2. There is the person that is an Action Taker: "Action Taker".
This person will listen to what you have to offer, if they like what you have they will be ready to do business, the action taker is always on the move, this is a doer, this person is sure of what they want, they know a good deal and a great product or service when they see or

hear about it. They are always ready to save money. This person is high energy, family minded, and executive or in management within business and might even own their own business.

3. You will meet the person who will need someone to help them make a decision The Supporter. "The Supporter" a wife, mother, very soft spoken, a very good listener, willing to give your product or service a try but will need to discuss it with her husband. It's best to find a good appointment time with this person and go back when both will have time to listen to your presentation, and they will need even more time to discuss it among themselves, but they will give you their decision.

4. Last but not least you will meet The Thinker: "The Thinker" will come to the door, ask you who you are what do you have and for the information, you might get about 2 minutes of their time. This person is a Business C.E.O. who has a family, plans everything they do, travels a lot and is always aware of every second of the day, and how it will be spent, you don't want to waste this person's time. However he will take your information and review it. You will need to ask when you can call or stop back by to see this person as they will take there time with their decision. Once you get an appointment with him don't miss it. You will not have another chance with this person. The good news is if they like what you have they will decide to purchase from you over 90% of the time.

Once you learn who you are talking to, it will be much easier to approach them with your products and services.
One thing that I learned very early in the business of sales is that you have to learn something about the people that you meet as you make contact to earn their business.

The way you approach people will make all of the difference in the world as to how they will respond to you. Ask yourself this question? What is it that I am going to be sharing with them? Know the answer to this question before you introduce yourself to them?

What does your body langue say about you? Are you approaching them with a smile from your entire being? Will they even feel it is ok to give you their time and attention? Are you a friendly person and can they feel safe in your presence. Sales people have the idea that they should be respected by the people they meet because the company they worked for hired them, but in the world of outside of the company you are just another person unknown and you have to command the time and respect of everyone you meet.

This is done by the way you carry yourself, and how you address the people you have to meet and greet on a daily basis. When we look at the people in our lives, family, friends, co-workers we can get a good idea of how we will be received by strangers and the prospects we greet everyday. Listen with your whole self when people are speaking to you, respond with good communication skills and always give clear and truthful answers about the subject matter in the conversation you have with them.

There are several kinds of people you will meet when you make sales calls or visits, and you have to remember that not a single one of them is waiting around for a sales person to ring their door bell or dial their phone number. This is why you have to be alert and on your toes with the very best tone and smile you have when they take time for you.

Yes you Mr. or Miss. sales person are an interruption, and you are not the important person when you make contact with people you have never met before, and what you have to offer is not even important to them it's your responsibility to let them know how much you appreciate their time and attention, your name and the company you work for, show them your company I.D. and let them respond to who you are first.

Then ask them and open ended question and give them time to answer you, If it's in your favor let them know that you have some good information about your company's products and services that may benefits them and their family. Ask for 5 minutes of their time, or when you might be able to set down with them and give them a short presentation to compare what you are offering to what they may have, and the benefits and saving they will receive as a result of doing business with you.

The Four Steps to Getting Buying Decisions for Your Products and Services.

The First Step:

Introduce yourself and the company you work with.

When I make a call or go up to a door of someone I am calling on for business I put a smile on my face, think about my opening greeting which I have already prepare before my arrival or call to the person. When they answer the phone or open the door I say hi Mr. or Miss. Williams I am Larry with XYZ Company, pause, and let them respond.

Look around if you are at their home, and make a comment on an award you may see, a car or truck in the drive way, the home itself

Get them talking about themselves and their accomplishments.

Once you have them comfortable with you move on to why you are there.

I am your area customer service consultant, and I stopped by today to meet you, and share some very important information about our products and services that may benefit you and your family, may I ask you a question? Make sure it is open ended, so they don't respond with a one word answer give them something to think about before they can respond to you.

Example: Mr. Williams may I ask you what has been your experience with your current service provider?

The second step:

   Listen To The Customer.

1. Listen to what the customer has to tell you about their experience, continue your discussion asking opened ended questions to discover needs and desires as well as ways your products and services can better serve their needs, also how you can make their experience much better with what you have to offer. Ask questions that will be use later in the sales call to assist you with your presentation when you set down with the customer to share with them how your products and services will give them more value for their investment dollars.

Once you have listened and make sure you take good notes written or mental so that you have a very clear understanding of what will help the customer have a better experience. Ask for about 5 minutes of their take to show them how what you have can improve that over all experience and save them money or give them more value for the services they are now paying for? Wait until they give you an answer, don't speak another word. When they respond then you speak. Looking for a yes answer go in and set down and give your presentation. If they say they don't have time right now, get an appointment.

Example: Mr. Williams I understand you are a busy man and time is important to you. May I ask you when would be a good time in the next two days for me to stop back by to speak with you? Sir would morning or afternoon by a better time? Let his answer you, write the date and time down. Thank him, also let him know you have enjoyed this learning experience, and you look forward to continue the discussion with him at the appointment date and time you have agreed to.

The Third Step:

The Presentation:

Make sure you know your products and services, this is where the rubber meets the road with the customer, and be ready to answer every question or make sure can get the answer while you are with the customer, this is no time for fumbling through the presentation, if you don't know it practice it over and over again and again until it's like a poem or sweet music coming off of your lips. Know your presentation and products and services.

First of all find out if your products and services are a fit for what the person is looking for. This is done by asking opened needs questions to find out needs and desires of the person. Once you know your product or service will work.

Share how your company is the best in the industry with a product or service demonstration of the effectiveness and quality of the service you will provide for the person. What they can expect to receive from your business in return for their investment dollars in your company.

Tell the customer how the product or service will benefit their needs.
 Go over the products features and benefits for the person, and how it will serve them, also tell them the benefits of having the product or service in their home.

Example: Mr. Williams this is our top of the line model and it will best serve your needs because this feature will do what you are looking for while you work on other projects and when you finish you can then review what you might have missed by touching the button here. This is how it works, and here are the benefits to having it in your home. Once you have finished your presentation, ask the customer if he have any questions? If so answer them, if not move on to the close.

Overcoming Objections and Handling the Close of the Sale:

Many sales people say this is the hardest part of the presentation, however it's really not hard at all. Once you have completed your presentation, answers all questions and concerns of your customer, the only thing left to do is close the sale.

He may also have an objection, welcome it, that's right and objection is the customers way of saying I am just about ready to do business, but I have a concern that has not been addressed yet. That's all an objection is.

Address the customer's objection concern by confirming you understand the objection, and responding to objection with a detailed answer to address it in your customer's favor. If you are unsure of the answer call someone and get an answer for the customer right then if possible and if not, assure the customer there is nothing to worry about and you will have an answer for him ASAP. In most cases this will not stop the decision to close the sale.

Handling the Close of the Sale:

Example:

Mr. Williams, now that we have answer all of your questions and concerns about our products and services, I just want to make sure you are happy with the presentation we have talked about together tonight? Mr. Williams will respond Yes? You reply very good sir.

Then ask him Mr. Williams, Sir how would you like to take care of your first month's service? Will you be using your Visa or Master Card? We also accept personal checks?

Don't you say another word until he responds to you. Who ever speaks first at this point in the sale will make the purchase of the product or service, and you don't want to spend all of this time to buy from yourself do you?

If he responds with a question answer it, and ask him again, sir will that be your Visa or Master card for your first monthly investment for our product or service.

You may close by asking Mr. Williams What day is good for us to do your installment of the product or service, I have Monday morning or Tuesday Afternoon open right now? Once again wait until he responds.

He make say I don't get paid for another two weeks and your response will be Mr. Williams that will be on the 20th is that correct? When he responds with yes, You say sir I can set your Installment date for the 21st in the morning or the 22nd in the afternoon, while date works better for you? Wait until he responds.

At that point if he is not ready to do business, kindly put your things away and thank him for his time, and ask his when will he be ready to move forward with the installment. Write it down and ask if you make call him two days before? Respond sir I will speak with you then. Give him your business card. And leave. Don't spend another minute of your time there. Move on to another appointment.

The Fourth Step:

Getting The Yes I Will Buy Decision From The Customer.

Until the customer makes a decision to purchase your products or services, you will not be able to complete the sales investment agreement forms and documentation.

Ask for their business, again, and again, and again, and if they say I have to think about it. Ask him, Mr. Williams is there a question you have that I may not have addressed? He may say yes or he may say no. when he responds to you, so be ready for his response.

If the answer is yes, answer the question, and ask for his business again.
If he says no, you want to ask him Mr. Williams what are your concerns at this time regarding what we have discussed about the products or services? How may I assist you in your decision to getting great quality service as a result having the best products or services on the market in your home in the next couple of days? Wait until he responds. Most of the time he will say okay lets go with your company.

Have every document and agreement needed ready to be completed you don't want to leave that room until every thing is completely finished and signed by the customer.

Set the appointment time: Mr. Williams when is a good time for our techs to do your installation of service? Would morning or afternoon be better for you? I Have Tuesday Morning or Wednesday afternoon?

Let him choose a time and date, and write it down. Give the customer all of his copies of the investment documentation, go over it with him and make sure he understands what he has purchased is what you discussed with him.

Set up a time to follow up with the customer when the installation is completed to be sure he is completely satisfied with the services and products he has purchased from you. Remember we never sell a customer they make a decision to purchase our products and services.

Thank the customer for their business and give them your contact information so you can be reached in event there is a question that may come up after you leave, or he may need to call you regarding the installation of the services and products.

Do your follow up and ask for referral business from the customer, the next customer may be a friend or family member of this one. Always keep in touch with your customers.

After a few days have past and you have made sure the customer is completely satisfied take a few seconds and send them a personal thank you note. Hand write it out on s blank card or a sheet of paper, mention something about them you remember during the conversation you had with them at the time of the purchase decision, make sure to print your name and contact information at the end of the note, and sign it and put in the mail. You must always be willing to re- invest back into your customers for their investment in products and services purchased from you and your company.

Dealing With Fear:

How can you become successful and over come the trials and troubles and fear that you are faced with everyday.

Fear is unforeseen things that appear to be real in our minds, 90% of our fear is only our mind playing trick on us. There is nothing to fear in sales, I always ask myself this question? What am I afraid of and why? When I know the answer my next question is, What will be the results if I don't overcome my fear and take action.

Will the pleasure of taking action out weight the fear I now have about what I am afraid to do? And the answer is always it's worth dealing with my fears if I'm going to be successful in sales. So I put the thing I fear in an imaginary box and say to it fear you wait right here I'll be back when I have closed my next appointment. Get out of my car walk up to my next appointment with a big smile on my face and knock on the door. Don't be defeated by what you fear.

10 Tips for Dealing with What You Fear.

1. Have faith in yourself.
2. Have a plan of action. What are your aspirations?
3. Stay focus on the results you are working to achieve.
4. Always live in the present and take care of what is right in front of you, don't worry about the past or the future, live each moment and enjoy being there in the present moment.
5. Share love with the people around you. Never let anger or hate stir within your heart, be filled with love, happiness, peace and laughter these good fruits at all times.
6. Work hard to achieve your dreams, goals, do this in small steps, some may say bite size pieces.
7. Stop to give thanks, always say thank you. 1st to your Creator for the wisdom and power to be the best and reach your goal; Being thankful is also the way you show our gratitude for the blessing we receive each day. Then to your customer for there time attention and purchase of your product and service. Finally to yourself for having the courage and not letting fear stand in the way helping someone who really needed to see you today.

8.   Never Quit, no matter how far down the road it is to your finish line, don't you dare quit; keep your eyes moving in front of you, only look back to say thanks for the progress you have made.

9.   Give back into the community, or business, of your time, talent, and resources, as you give you will receive much more than you will ever give to others.

10.   Always Give Quality Service: the way people view your business will have a direct reflection on you.

Business Success Prayer:

A friend sent me this prayer a few years ago, I started to pray it everyday, so let me share with you.

"I recognize the eternal source of all riches which never fails. I am divinely guided in all my ways, and I adapt myself to all new ideas. Infinite intelligence is constantly revealing to me better ways to serve my fellow man. I am guided and directed to provide products that will bless and help humanity. I attract men and women who are spiritual, loyal, faithful, and talented, and who contribute to the peace, prosperity, and the progress of our business. I am an irresistible magnet and attract fabulous wealth by giving the best possible quality products and services.

I am constantly in tune with the infinite and the substance of wealth. In finite intelligence governs all my plans and purposes, and I predicate all my success on the truth that God leads, guides, and governs me in all my undertakings. I am at peace inwardly and outwardly at all times. I am a tremendous success. I am one with God, and God is always successful. I must succeed. I am succeeding now. I grasp the essentials of all details of my business. I radiate love and goodwill to all details of my business, to all those around me and to all my employees and associates. I fill my mind and heart with God's love, power and energy. All those connected with me are spiritual links in my growth, welfare and prosperity. I give all honor and glory to God"

This business tycoon brought all these things he desired in his life to pass, so he wanted you to be blessed just as he has been, so pass this prayer on to your friends and love ones.

Author unknown.

In this modern world of the gadget and electronics, cell phones, ipads, lap top computers, email marketing , iphones, Androids, Xboxes, Play Stations, and so much more, many people still appreciate the sale person who is willing to go the extra mile and come to their home take a seat and give them a real presentation of their company's products and services. Nothing takes the place of good salesmanship and quality superior customer service even in today's world.

I want to say thank you for spending time with me today and reviews many of the things you already know, however as all good green grass is healthy so are the minds of sales people who take the time to drink

fresh water from the wells of their peers and sales leaders.
The end.